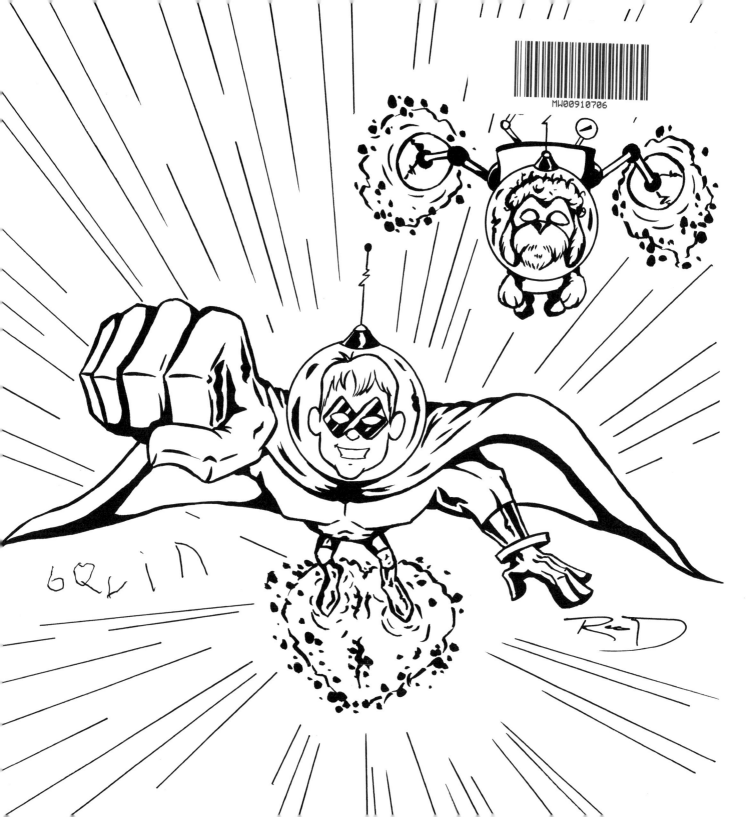

"Mighty Mito Superhero"

Mighty Mito
SUPERHERO

written by

Makenzie Lawrey

Hi! My name is Makenzie and I am writing this book in honor of my little brother Gavin. Gavin has a Mitochondrial Disease. Not many people know about Mito and there is no cure. I have hope that I can help raise awareness and raise money to find a cure so that people like my brother won't have to suffer anymore. Mito is killing more children than all pediatric cancers combined. It's time we find a cure!

I love my little brother Gavin because he is so brave. He goes through more tests than most adults do and he doesn't even cry. He is my hero. My wish is that he could be better and live like normal kids do. Seeing him sick all the time makes me sad.

I would like to dedicate this book to my superhero brother, Gavin.

In honor of all the Mito Warriors and Mito Angels.

Especially these three who have touched my heart:
My brother Gavin, my friend Xavier,
and sweet Rylee.

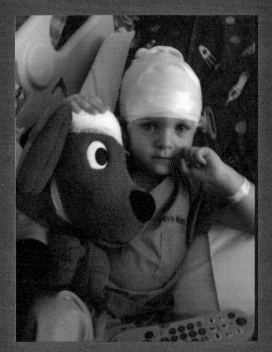

Mito kids are brave; they are like superheroes. I am going to tell you about a special little boy named Gavin and the disease that has changed his and our entire family's life. He has Mitochondrial Disease and there is no cure. Gavin has to go to the doctors and hospital all the time, but he stays strong and brave and that's why I call him my superhero.

Let me tell you about Mitochondrial Disease. First of all, it's a long word... so we call it Mito for short. Mitochondria lives in all the cells in our body except our red blood cells. That means it lives in our heart, our brain, our stomach muscle, our lungs and more. Mitochondria gives us energy. Mitochondria are responsible for creating more than 90% of the energy the body needs to grow and sustain life. Mitochondria is like a battery for humans; it's what keeps us going. Eventually batteries start to fade. If you have a mitochondrial disease, it is like a battery that's dying because mitochondria start to die off. There are thousands of mitochondria in our body. As they die off, our bodies and organs weaken and could die. Think about what happens when a battery dies in a toy. The toy doesn't work anymore. When you have Mito, the same thing happens to your body and organs. Your mitochondria start to die like a battery does, and then your body and organs don't work right anymore.

Most people don't know what Mitochondrial Disease is, but they should because the mighty mitochondria produce energy for our bodies to function and move. Everyone eats food and drinks water to give our bodies energy. We need energy to help our bodies move, just like a car gets energy when you put gas in it. The gas goes to the engine of a car and makes energy to move the car's wheels. Use your imagination and pretend your body is a car and your mitochondria is the engine. When you eat food it is like putting gas in your car. The food turns into energy to help your body move just like the gas changes into energy to help the car move. Imagine if your car ran out of gas, it wouldn't run anymore. Gavin's mitochondria in his body isn't working very well. He cannot make as much energy as other kids. Gavin tires very easily.

There are over forty different types of Mito. Even if two people have the same type of Mito, they can still have very different symptoms. Doctors have a difficult time diagnosing people with Mito because their symptoms are so different. Plus, many doctors don't even know what Mito is! Gavin started to show symptoms at one and a half years old. Even though he went through A LOT of tests at the doctors and spent a lot of time in the hospital, it still took four years before we knew he had Mito.

When Gavin was a baby, he was like a normal baby. He was happy and healthy. He was really smart too. When I was in kindergarten, he would stand behind me when I was practicing my reading flash cards and he would yell out the words before me. I was so surprised that he knew the words I was still trying to learn. He was only two! Now he's six and repeating kindergarten. His brain struggles to think sometimes because of his Mito. Now he only knows fifteen words. When he was two, he knew over forty words. This makes me sad for him and makes me feel like other kids are doing better than him. He has a hard time in school and it's not his fault; it's Mito's fault.

Gavin's entire life changed in just a few weeks, but like many Mito families, we didn't know what was wrong. He first started to have hand tremors (I call them shakies) when he was eighteen-months-old. The tremors were the first symptom of Gavin's disease. We found out he has a movement disorder. His shakies were just in his hands at first, then they got worse and were in his whole body. Sometimes shaking makes it hard for him to eat because he can't get his food in his mouth. Other times, he cannot walk by himself because his whole body is shaky. One of the things that makes Gavin so special is that even when his legs are so shaky he can't walk, he doesn't cry or get mad. Instead, he will be silly and while he is laughing, he will say to our mom, "Will you help me? My legs aren't working again." In situations where most kids would be scared, Gavin is always brave.

Soon after we found out Gavin was having shakies he started to have seizures. A seizure is like a thunderstorm in your brain. A seizure means your brain is not communicating right. When your brain doesn't communicate the right way, there are many different things that can happen because there are many different types of seizures. Sometimes, Gavin has what we call a silent seizure. When he has those, he won't answer us and he stares off into space. Sometimes when this happens, I don't realize he is having a silent seizure and I think he is ignoring me. But he's really not. He also has Grand Mal

seizures , which make you really convulsive, and his eyes usually roll in the back of his head. He's usually pretty confused afterward and doesn't remember them. They are really scary to watch. Gavin often hurts himself when he has Grand Mal seizures and has even had to go to the hospital. Gavin's seizures are also caused by his Mito.

Gavin has a seizure alert dog named Hershey because of all of his seizures. Hershey is a black toy poodle with a funny white beard. He is Gavin's service animal. Hershey is a "working" dog and goes everywhere with Gavin, even to school and the hospital. His job is to help take care of Gavin by letting us know before Gavin has a seizure. He usually gives us a three-to-five minute warning by jumping up and down, tugging on ours and Gavin's clothes and licking us like crazy! Hershey works hard all the time and takes care of Gavin, but is also always by Gavin's side and is Gavin's best friend. When Gavin is in the hospital, he gets bored and likes to play tricks on the nurses. He hides Hershey in the stuffed animals and tells him to "stay" and then hits the call button for the nurse. When they come in, he will tap Hershey without the nurse seeing and Hershey jumps out of the stuffed animals and scares them.
Gavin thinks this is so funny.

A lot of people wonder how Hershey knows BEFORE Gavin is going to have a seizure. Dogs can smell things that people can't because they have a really good sense of smell. When someone is going to have a seizure, their body gives off a different scent that Hershey was trained to pick up on. So, how it works is that Gavin, like everyone else, has a "normal" scent and then when he is going to have a seizure, he has a seizure scent that the dog trainers told us smells sweet and fruity to a dog. When Hershey smells that scent, he knows that he needs to alert us that Gavin is going to have a seizure soon. Now that we have Hershey, we always know when Gavin is going to have a seizure and we can get him in a safe place so he doesn't get hurt as much anymore. Gavin is my Superhero, and Hershey is Gavin's Superhero!

People aren't used to seeing a seizure alert dog or a service animal that is as small as Hershey. So, sometimes people look at us weird or make rude comments and then my parents politely explain that Hershey is a service dog and we continue walking. Other times, businesses tell my Mom and Dad that we can't go into certain places because we have a dog with us. Then, we have to explain that Hershey is a service animal.

There are a lot of different types of working dogs. A seizure alert dog is just one type of working dog. Another type of working dog that I think is cool is a dog that works with the police. They are called "K-9's". These dogs are specifically trained to help assist police and other law-enforcement officials in their work. One of the most common types of working dog is a guide dog, which is used by blind people. These dogs help people who can't see. They're specially trained dogs that help them know where they're going, so they don't hurt themselves. Often times, people think Hershey is a guide dog because they aren't used to seeing seizure alert dogs. Sometimes people will say things about Gavin being blind because they assume Hershey is a guide dog. One time at school, a fifth grader said to his friend, "you can't touch that little boy's dog because he's blind!" Gavin yelled in a silly voice, "I'm not blind! I can see you!" The fifth grade boy was shocked and didn't know what to say. He walked away quickly and ran up the stairs. It's important for people to know that there are lots of different types of service animals with different jobs to help people with whatever their needs are.

Hershey isn't the only one who helps Gavin, other people do too. I like to help Gavin so he feels safe, and so he doesn't use up all his energy. One of the things I do to help is I clean his room, even though no one asks me to and I really don't like it, but I do it anyway so that Gavin can save his energy for important stuff. Another thing I do to help is I hold his hand when he gets his blood drawn and when he gets shaky. One time, in the middle of the night, I saw the bathroom light on and got up to see who it was. It was Gavin in the bathroom and he was shaky. I sat on the floor and had him sit on my lap so he wouldn't fall. I put my arms around him and said, "Be quiet so we don't wake up Mommy. She needs her sleep. I will take care of you." My Mom heard us talking and woke up anyway because she can hear everything!

The person who helps Gavin the most is my Mom. My Mom is like a hero to our family because she quit her job to take care of Gavin full-time. She doesn't sleep very well

because she worries about Gavin. Gavin shakes, has seizures and is in a lot of pain at night time. Gavin doesn't sleep very well at night time either and sometimes has a hard time falling asleep. To help him calm down at night, he likes my Mom to rub his face and back while singing and humming to him. Sometimes in the middle of the night, she will get up and rock him in the rocking chair.

During the day, my Mom goes to school with Gavin as Hershey's handler. After school, Gavin takes a nap to regain some energy and then my mom takes him to his therapy and doctor appointments. Gavin has to be hospital homebound because he is too weak to be at school all day because of his Mito. He has a tutor who comes two times a week and then my Mom works with him and helps him get caught up

on school work the other days. My Mom also gives him all his morning and afternoon medicine. He takes a lot of medicine. One of the other things she does to take good care of Gavin is stay with him the whole time he is in the hospital. My Daddy usually stays with me to help me feel safe.

My Dad helps our entire family by going to work every day and working really hard to support us all. Having Mito is really expensive! He is really good at helping Gavin to be brave during difficult times. One time Gavin had to have surgery on his head, so we shaved his head at home before he had to go to the hospital. We shaved it as a family so that it didn't seem scary to Gavin. I even got to shave his head myself! I started with a mohawk and after we all laughed. Then my Mom and I shaved the rest together. My Dad is 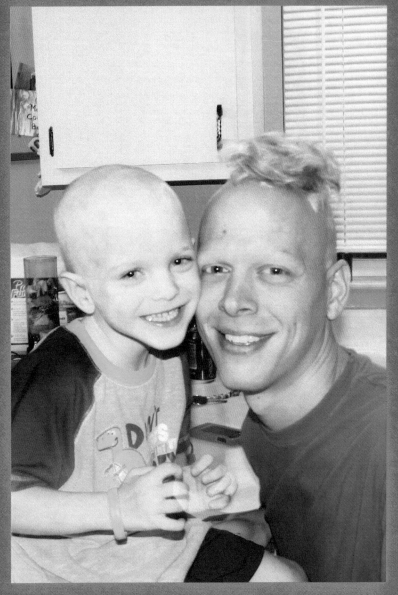 bald and sometimes I like to call him "Baldy". After we cut all of Gavin's hair off, Gavin thought it would be funny to put his pile of blonde hair on my Dad's head.

My Dad also helps me to be brave when Gavin is sick. He always takes me to visit Gavin when he is in the hospital as long as he is not at a hospital far away. Visiting Gavin always makes me feel better because I can see him and see how he is doing. Gavin was in the hospital for Easter one time, so my Dad and I brought him an Easter basket and I helped him open it. Then my Dad hid Easter eggs around his hospital room for us to find and we both loved it. Then, another time, Gavin was in the hospital for Thanksgiving, so my Dad and I made a big Thanksgiving dinner at home. This was the first time I got to make an entire holiday meal and we cooked all day long. Even though Gavin was really sick that holiday and we had to wear special masks in order to visit him, we did our best to still enjoy our special dinner as a family.

Gavin takes lots of medicine to help with all the different problems he has from his Mito. Mitochondrial disease affects your entire body in many different ways. The disease causes the most damage to your brain, heart, muscles and lungs. The reason these are the parts of your body that are affected the most is because they need the most energy.

There are a lot of terrible things that Mito does to a person. Strokes, seizures, severe vomiting, constipation, diarrhea, swallowing difficulties, blindness, deafness, heart and kidney problems, muscle failure, heat/cold intolerance, difficulties growing, diabetes, lactic acidosis, immune system problems and liver disease are just some of them. And one of the scary things about Mito is not knowing how Mito is going to affect you. Gavin's Mito Doctor told us not to compare Gavin to other Mito kids and to look at this as "Gavin's Mito". You never know what to expect, what will happen next or how aggressive Gavin's Mito is and that's scary.

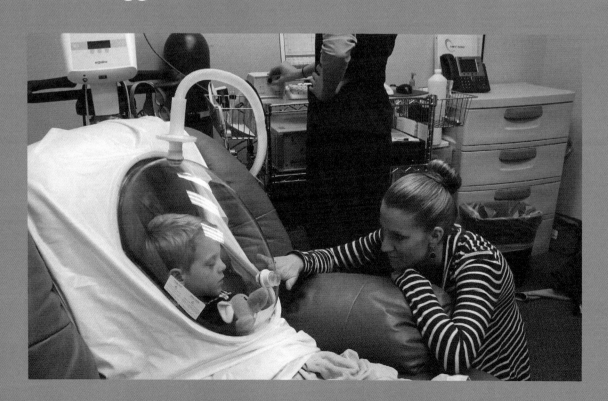

One of the things that have already been greatly affected on Gavin are his lungs. There are different types of muscles in our bodies. Some are known as smooth muscles. One type of smooth muscle is found in our lungs. Our lungs are part of our respiratory system. These muscles are called cilia. The cilia muscles are smaller than little hairs. In a healthy person, the silly little cilia play all day and are always on the move. They love to play catch with the particles we breathe in, just like kids like to play catch with their dads. The particles are like a baseball that you throw back and forth. When our silly cilia catch the particles we breathe in, they throw them to another cilia muscle.

Unfortunately, Gavin's silly cilia are weak because of Gavin's Mito and they forget to throw the particles back and forth. So Gavin has to use this special piece of medical equipment called an Airway Vest Cleansing Machine. It kind of looks like a life vest that you use when you swim. The vest fills with air and shakes Gavin up. This helps Gavin's silly cilia move like they are supposed to and helps keep him from getting lung infections as often. Gavin likes to talk and sing when he has the vest on because it makes his voice sound weird and shaky.

The airway vest cleansing system isn't the only machine that Gavin uses everyday. He also uses a nebulizer to help with his lungs. Gavin gets a lot of lung infections and easily becomes short of breath due to the effects of Mito on his lungs. Breathing takes a lot of work, but if you don't have Mito, you may not realize how much energy it takes. There is a muscle in our body just under our lungs. That muscle is called the diaphragm. When the diaphragm moves, it allows air to come into our lungs, that is what breathing is. The doctor put Gavin on a BIPAP machine to make it so Gavin can breath easier at night time. We hope that while Gavin is resting, his diaphragm is too.

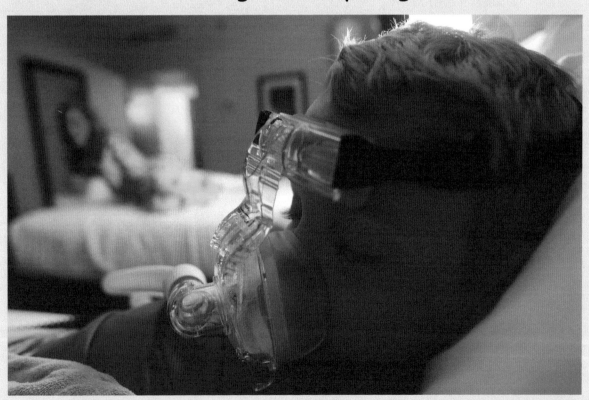

Gavin's entire body needs to rest often. If he runs and plays for too long like the rest of the kids his age, he gets short of breath, his face gets really pale and he becomes shaky. If he plays too hard one day, he will end up very sore at night time and has to take extra pain medicine and use A LOT of ice packs to try to feel better.

Gavin is already sick enough. I know that without a cure, he could still get worse. Many people don't understand that even when Gavin looks healthy on the outside, his body is still sick on the inside. It's important for people to understand that even on Gavin's good days and no matter how "good" he looks, on the inside his cells are causing him pain and muscle weakness. Because of his Mito, he has some really yucky days. But because he's an amazing little boy, he still has some really awesome days too. On a good day, Gavin enjoys taking pictures with my Mom's fancy camera, pretending to be the Green Power Ranger, all while singing and dancing with a goofy grin on his face. I want my brother and all the people with Mito to have a future filled with hope for a cure.

Credits:

Front and back cover art illustrated by Phil Rood under the direction of 5-year-old Mito Warrior Gavin Lawrey

Cartoon Illustrations done by Phil Rood (pages 5, 6, 7, 9, 12, 14, 19, 22 & 26)

Photography by Shannon Jordan Dodge Photography (pages 13 & 27)

Photography by Vera Camaj Photography (page 1)

Photography by Sarah Coward, Photojournalist for The News-Press (pages 17, 20, 21, 23, 24 & 25)

Family Photos (pages 4, 8, 10, 11, 15 & 18)

A special thank you to Dr. Jose Colon for his guidance, medical knowledge, and for being Gavin's ever-present champion.

We also appreciate Jamie Ayres & Cristela Guerra for continued support.

Made in the USA
Lexington, KY
31 January 2014